MINDFULNESS WHILE

RUNNING ERRANDS

PRISCILLA AN

childsworld.com

The Child's World®
childsworld.com

Published by The Child's World®
800-599-READ · www.childsworld.com

Photography Credits
Photographs ©: iStockphoto, cover, 1, 5, 7, 8–9, 11, 12; Trong Nguyen/Shutterstock Images, 3; M Studio Images/iStockphoto, 14–15, 16, 19, 20; Wave Break Media/Shutterstock Images, 22

ISBN Information
9781503869684 (Reinforced Library Binding)
9781503880931 (Portable Document Format)
9781503882249 (Online Multi-user eBook)
9781503883550 (Electronic Publication)
9781645498681 (Paperback)

LCCN 2022951171

Printed in the United States of America

Priscilla An is a children's book editor and author. She lives in Minnesota with her rabbit and likes to practice mindfulness through yoga.

TABLE OF CONTENTS

WHAT IS MINDFULNESS?

Running **errands** with an adult can sometimes feel boring. Walking around can be tiring. People can easily get **distracted** by all the sights. Practicing mindfulness can be helpful. Mindfulness is when people are aware of their thoughts, feelings, and surroundings. Being mindful while running errands can help people **focus** on the present moment. It can help people be **patient**. Practicing mindfulness can make running errands fun!

Helping parents run errands can be fun.

THE PRESENT MOMENT

Harper is grumpy. Her dad woke her up early this morning. She wanted to sleep late. But he wanted to take her to a holiday market. He said they needed to find a gift for her mom. Harper is not happy to be outside in the cold. She hugs her dad's arm as they walk through the market. "Can you just carry me?" she complains. "I'm tired."

It is important for people to wear warm clothes in cold weather.

Shopping for the holidays can be tiring but fun.

"Would a donut help you feel less tired?" Harper's dad asks. He points to a donut stand. "I know how much you like them." Harper perks up. She runs to the stand and picks a frosted donut with sprinkles. She takes a big bite.

"Mm, it's so good," Harper says with a full mouth. Her dad laughs.

"What does it taste like?" he asks.

"Like a birthday cake and cereal mixed together!" Harper shouts.

Harper is happy with her donut. But after a while, she starts to feel impatient. She wants to go home. Harper watches her dad look at some necklaces.

"Can we just get mom some candy?" she asks. "I think she will really like it." Harper points at a big lollipop.

"Harper," her dad says, "I think that's what *you* want. Giving gifts means thinking of what the other person wants."

Harper pouts. She knows her dad is right. She just feels bored! She wants to go home.

"How about we try something together? It might help you feel less tired and bored," her dad says.

"What is it?" Harper asks.

"Focus on your senses. Tell me what you smell, hear, feel, and see," her dad says.

"OK," Harper sighs. She **inhales** deeply. "I smell pine trees and donuts. I also smell my shampoo." She then pauses to listen to her surroundings. "I hear people talking and cars driving. And I feel. . ." Harper closes her eyes. Then she gasps. "Something cold is falling on me!" Her eyes fly open. "It's snowing!" She tilts her head up to the sky. A couple of snowflakes rest on her eyelashes before they disappear.

Snow sometimes feels magical.

As she watches the snow fall, Harper remembers something her mom said. "Dad, can we buy mom a new scarf? She said she wants a new one. It will be super important when we play in the snow!"

"Great idea," her dad exclaims. He gives Harper a big hug. "Let's go find your mom a warm scarf!"

MINDFUL GIFTS

Giving gifts is a way people can practice mindfulness. Before people give gifts, they can pay attention to the other person's likes and dislikes. Gifts do not have to cost money. People can give personal gifts, such as drawings or handwritten letters.

People can find exciting gifts at markets.

Harper and her dad find the perfect scarf. They even pick out a small Christmas tree! Harper is excited for her mom to see her gift. She will be so surprised.

Harper felt tired and grumpy at first. But practicing mindfulness helped her stay in the present moment. It made running errands feel less boring. Instead of wanting to go home, Harper felt excited to feel, smell, and listen to the things around her.

PAYING ATTENTION

Ezra goes to the farmer's market with his mom every Sunday morning. He does not like running errands with his mom. She always takes such a long time. He usually brings a toy to play with. But he forgot one today.

A typical farmer's market sells many fruits and vegetables.

Running errands
may feel boring.

Ezra drags his feet as his mom moves from **stall** to stall. He wishes his mom would take him somewhere fun, like a candy store. Instead, he is stuck waiting for his mom in between stalls of fruits and vegetables.

"Mom, I am *so* bored," Ezra groans. "Are you almost done?" He pulls on the sleeve of his mom's sweater.

"Why are you bored?" Ezra's mom asks.

"I have nothing to do. We do the same thing every Sunday. Nothing changes," Ezra whines.

Ezra's mom brings him to a stall with fresh fruits for sale. She picks up a basket of strawberries. "All the fruits here came freshly picked from a plant or tree. Take a look at these. Did you see strawberries last week?"

Ezra tries thinking back to the week before. "I don't think so."

"That's right! Strawberries were not ready yet last week. But now, they're in **season**. That means we will see more of them at the market," his mom says.

A woman behind the stall smiles. "Do you want to try one?"

Ezra nods. When he takes a bite, he is amazed. The strawberry tastes so juicy and sweet. It is almost like candy!

"Every Sunday is different," Ezra's mom says. "Every moment is different. Something is always happening. You just have to pay attention. Then you might feel less bored." She takes Ezra's hand. "For the rest of our time here, try focusing on the things that are different."

SEASONAL FRUITS

People can find most fruits at the grocery store all year long. But fruits are in season at different times. Fruits that are in season usually taste fresher. They also might have more flavor. Eating seasonal fruits can help people be mindful of the passing of time.

Eating a snack can help energize people when they feel tired.

People can see and buy different things at a farmer's market.

As they walk, Ezra starts to look around. He finds a new stall that is selling jars of honey. As his mom passes a bakery stall, Ezra sees freshly baked blueberry muffins. They smell good!

When it is time for them to go home, Ezra is surprised. Time passed by so quickly this time. He was no longer bored. For the first time, Ezra is excited to run errands with his mom next Sunday. He cannot wait to see what has changed at the market!

WONDER MORE

Wondering about New Information

How much did you know about mindfulness while running errands before reading this book? What new information did you learn? Write down two new facts that this book taught you. Was the new information surprising? Why or why not?

Wondering How It Matters

What is one way being mindful while running errands relates to your life? How do you think it relates to other kids' lives?

Wondering Why

Focusing on your senses can help you be more mindful. Why might this be so? How might knowing this affect your life?

Ways to Keep Wondering

Learning about mindfulness can be a complex topic. After reading this book, what questions do you have about it? What can you do to learn more about it?

STRETCH TO SUCCESS

Running errands with an adult can sometimes mean a lot of walking. Stretching can help your body feel less tired. Try these two stretches before or during an errand.

Arm Circles

1. Hold your arms out to your sides, making a straight line.

2. Draw circles with your arms. Start by making small circles. Then make bigger circles.

3. Rotate your arms in both directions. Move slowly so you do not get hurt or hit people around you.

Neck Stretches

1. Lean your head toward your right shoulder.

2. Then, slowly lean your head toward your left shoulder.

3. Look down. Make sure your chin is touching your chest. Then, slowly look up.

4. Repeat these movements. Remember to move slowly so you do not get hurt!

GLOSSARY

distracted (dih-STRAKT-ed) When people are distracted, they are not able to pay attention to a task. Ezra was so distracted by the thought of being bored that he did not notice interesting things around him.

errands (EH-runds) Errands are trips to get something done. Going to the grocery store or the bank are examples of errands.

focus (FOH-kuss) To focus is to pay special attention to something. People are practicing mindfulness when they focus on their senses.

inhales (in-HAYLS) When a person inhales, she is breathing in. Harper inhales and notices what she smells.

patient (PAY-shunt) Being patient means staying calm while waiting. People may have to be patient when running errands.

season (SEE-zuhn) When food is in season, it means it is the time of year when the food is freshest. At the farmer's market, Ezra found out that strawberries were in season.

stall (STAHL) A stall is a booth or a stand where people sell things. Ezra saw a stall that was selling blueberry muffins.

FIND OUT MORE

In the Library

An, Priscilla. *Mindfulness and Pets.*
Parker, CO: The Child's World, 2024.

DiOrio, Rana. *What Does It Mean to Be Present?*
Naperville, IL: Little Pickle Press, 2017.

Lawler, Jean C. *How Quiet-Time Makes You Feel.*
Egremont, MA: Red Chair Press, 2019.

On the Web

Visit our website for links about mindfulness while running errands:
childsworld.com/links

Note to Parents, Caregivers, Teachers, and Librarians: We routinely verify our Web links to make sure they are safe and active sites. So encourage your readers to check them out!

INDEX